SMOKE ON THE MEADOW

SELECTED LYRICS 1977 - 2017

SMOKE ON THE MEADOW
SELECTED LYRICS 1977 - 2017

CHRISTOPHER MARK JONES

FIRST EDITION

Little Red Tree Publishing, LLC,
509 W 3rd Street, North Platte, NE 69101

Copyright © 2017 Christopher Mark Jones

All rights are reserved under International and Pan-American Copyright Conventions. Except for brief passages quoted in a newspaper, magazine, radio or television review, no part of this book may be reproduced in any form or by any means, electronic or mechanical, including photocopying and recording, or by any information storage and retrieval system, without permission in writing from the publisher.

Layout and Cover Design: Michael Linnard, MCSD
Times New Roman, Minion Pro, Arial, Gils Sans, and Bell MT.

First Edition, 2017, manufactured in USA
1 2 3 4 5 6 7 8 9 10 LSI 23 22 21 20 19 18 17

Photographs on page viii, x, and 134, by Linda Benedict-Jones.
Photography on page xii by Ruth Hendrix.

All CD Cover designs and photos by Christopher Mark Jones, pages 2, 4, 6, 8, 10, 11, 12, 13, 14, 16, 20, 22, 24, 25, 26, 28, 29, 30, 32, 34, 35, 38, 40, 42, 44, 48, 50, 52, 54, 56, 58, 60, 62, 64, 66, 68, 72, 74, 76, 78, 80, 82, 84, 86, 88, 90, 94, 96, 98, 100, 104, 108, 110, 114, 116, 118, 120, 122.

Library of Congress Cataloging-in-Publication Data

Names: Jones, Christopher Mark., author.
Title: Smoke on the Meadow: Selected Lyrics 1977-2017 / by Christopher Mark Jones
Description: First edition. | North Platte, NE : Little Red Tree
  Publishing, 2017. | Includes discography
Identifiers: LCCN 2017056552 | ISBN 9781935653500 (pbk. : alk. paper)
Subjects: LCSH: Song Lyrics
Classification: LCC PS3573.I4787 A6 2017 | DDC 811/.54--dc23
LC record available at https://lccn.loc.gov/2017056552

Little Red Tree Publishing LLC
509 W 3rd Street,
North Platte, NE 69101
www.littleredtree.com

Contents

Introduction by Christopher Mark Jones	xi
The sun sets on the prairie	1
Dust To Dust	2
Rock County Line	4
The Trapper's Wife	6
Kansas	8
Hard To Imagine	10
The Dakota Territory	11
Holy	12
Gas It Up	13
A Question of Style	14
Black Earth	16
This whole world's my lover	22
The World Rolls On	20
What That Means	22
Railway Track	24
Best I Got	25
High	26
Hockey Éternité	28
Hockey Eternity [Hockey Éternité]	29
Whatever You Do	30
Don't Look Behind	32
Cincinnati Night	34
Walkin' 19	35
The sweet sound of lawnmowers	36
Mrs. Pennington	38
Drivin'	40
Home At Last	42
Suburban 2-Step	44

I saw the sea come slowly rising   47

    Lordstown   48
    Big Mac   50
    Steelhead Blues   52
    All They Seek   54
    The Blackstone Rangers   56
    Roseland   58
    Miguel y Celestina   60
    Hoop Dreams   62
    Dans La Ville   64
    In the City [Dans La Ville]   66
    I Saw the Sea Come Slowly Rising   68

You spoke to me with fingertips   71

    Spoken For   72
    Love's Not a Fashion   74
    Yes   76
    I'll Stay By Your Side   78
    Muffins   80
    Morning Glory   82
    Ballerina   84
    Bobby & Ginnie   86
    Road To Spain   88
    Field of Dreams   90

The trail of lost and found   93

    The Fire So Soon   94
    Uncertain Times   96
    No More Range To Roam   98
    Autumn Song   100
    I Work Hard For a Living   102
    Incantations   104
    C'est Pas Pour Moi   106
    It's Not For Me [C'est Pas Pour Moi]   108
    The Numbers   110

Appendix A: Discography of Christopher
    Mark Jones recordings   113
About the Author   124

Christopher Mark Jones, on the road, somewhere in France, 1975. Photo by Linda Benedict-Jones.

Acknowledgement

Michael Linnard and I have a relationship that covers roughly the span of this selection, begun when he signed on in 1976 to travel with me as a backup guitarist throughout the U.K. and northern Europe. When he suggested that Little Red Tree would be a possible venue for producing a book of lyrics, it only took five years or so to follow up on his suggestion.

Each recording of these songs carries a complete set of acknowledgements, which I will not repeat here. The origin of anything I've done in music can no doubt be traced back to my parents William and Audrey, and my siblings James, Jeffrey and Karen, musicians all, who support and critique each other's efforts. The foundation of my adult life continues to be my wife and partner Linda Benedict-Jones, without whom the range of this selection would be unimaginable.

Michael Linnard, Christopher and Jeffrey Jones. Amsterdam, 1977. Photo by Linda Benedict-Jones.

Introduction

Songwriting is a short form, like haiku or flash fiction, that demands an efficient recounting of whatever's on the table, using components like a verse and chorus, a bridge (a mid-song variation), and usually rhyme. Liberties with all of these are allowed, and often taken.

Subject matter tends toward the sentiments, but this is a matter of choice, depending on a songwriter's current state of mind and relationships. Like any narrative form, songs also allow for adopting alternate points of view as a way of attempting to portray existence from outside our individual bubbles. In my case, I've written from the point of view of a single mother, a black teenager, an auto worker, and many others, including my own.

I have been writing songs since my teenage years. The songs in this volume constitute a thread begun during periods of living in Paris, London, Boston and most recently Pittsburgh, where I now live. Written mostly on acoustic guitar, they can loosely be described as pertaining to the folk genre. Other songs, including an entire repertoire written during fruitful years as the leader of an electric band in Boston, are not represented here.

Songs have allowed me to express myself concerning the many worlds that my life has touched, to interact with listeners and fellow musicians, and to continuously challenge myself to be creative. Songs are built of words and music, of course, and a book presents only the words. The combined form is still available for all of these songs; feel free to explore further should the spirit move you.

Christopher Mark Jones, 2017

Christopher Mark Jones at the Club Cafe, Pittsburgh 2013. Photo Ruth Hendrix.

The sun sets on the prairie

Dust to Dust

Woke up this mornin' in a strange light
The sun was a rusty brown
Nothin' movin' anywhere
Weeds lyin' dead on the ground

I could hear my youngest cryin'
Dirt all around her mouth
Screen door slappin' in the steady wind
Burnin' up from the south

Alice get the children
We're headin' for distant lands
All we can do is keep movin' and singin'
To the rhythm of the pots and pans

This ground's a cold woman
Make you feel like a fool
Ain't no use diggin'
All you do is break your tool

I spent my life workin' this earth
Hopin' somethin' would finally come
It's like preachin' the gospel to a congregation
Of the deaf and dumb

Alice get the children
We're headin' for distant lands
All we can do is keep movin' and singin'
To the rhythm of the pots and pans

California may not be paradise
There's a lot out there to fear
But I've got nothin' left to lose
And it's too goddam dusty here.

Alice get the children
We're headin' for distant lands
All we can do is keep movin' and singin'
To the rhythm of the pots and pans
Movin' and singin'
Movin' and singin'
Movin' and singin'
To the rhythm of the pots and pans

Rock County Line

I'll go walking that Rock County line
This was my father's, but it's not mine
Now it's a Walmart and a parking lot
The land is gone, I'm not sure what we got

Ellis island and the railway west
Black earth homesteads in a row
Harvest plenty led to books and schools
Then the children rose to go

I'll go walking that Rock County line
This was my mother's, but it's not mine
We once were farmers and now we're not
The farms are gone, I'm not sure what we got

Football and cars were my lucky stars
Then the GM plant second shift
I hunted fished and raised a family
I guess you'd say I got my wish

So I'll go walking that Rock County line
This was my father's, but it's not mine
Now it's a Walmart and a parking lot
The land is gone, I'm not sure what we got

I heard the doctor say I'll soon be gone
It doesn't really matter why
I'm done with night shifts, done with grease and noise
I'll soon belong to open sky.

So I'm out walking that Rock County line
This was my mother's, but it's not mine
We once were farmers and now we're not
The farms are gone, I'm not sure what I got

So I'm out walkin' that Rock County line
Out walkin' that Rock County line

The Trapper's Wife

She pulled right over and picked me up
Asked me Where you goin' tonight?
I said I might make it to Black Earth
If the wind keeps blowin' just right

She said That's nice but I turn off
At the top of the next rise
If you want you can stay the night
There's no need to act surprised

My house is a little worse for wear
There's traps and snowshoes piled up everywhere
Used to have a man to share my bed
But it's been seven long years now
That he's been dead.

I said All right it's gettin' on dark
And the trucks don't stop up here
I could use a bite to eat
And some Pabst Blue Ribbon beer

She said Don't get happy
Your bed is a pile of skins
Last week's stew is almost gone
And the moonshine is runnin' thin

My head is a little worse for wear
There's dusty memories tucked in everywhere
Used to have a man to share my bed
But it's been seven long years now
That he's been dead

We stopped in at the Texaco
She came out with the Pabst
Stacked it up on the muskrat hides
Between the gas cans in the back

She said Heat some water on the wood stove
You don't smell that good
In the dark we didn't talk much
We just did what we could

Morning come she drove me down to the highway
Dropped me at roadside
Said I'm Joline not that it matters
What matters is what's inside

My heart is a little worse for wear
All these old love songs, tangled everywhere
Used to have a man to share my bed
Now there's a new song playing
In my house, in my heart, in my head

There's a new song playing
In my house, in my heart, and in my head

Kansas

I don't have friends
I got buddies
I keep my boots on
Even when they're muddy

All the sweet things
They call me honey
They treat me so nice
While they're taking my money

I was born here in Kansas
And this is where I'll stay
It may not be heaven
But it sure does feel that way

I stop in at Quicker Liquor
On a Saturday night
Or head down to Hog Heaven
For some ribs and Bud Light

My truck is two-tone
Red on top, dust on the bottom
You want some back seats
Well, you know that I ain't got 'em

I was born here in Kansas
And this is where I'll stay
It may not be heaven
But it sure does feel that way

If we're not out on the rigs
We'll be out on the range
We can tell you're not from here
If you think that's strange

Some like the shorthorns
I like the long
Jesus rules the radio
I'm right where I belong

I was born here in Kansas
And this is where I'll stay
It may not be heaven
But it sure does feel that way

Hard to Imagine

The sun is settin' on a Midwestern town
The kids are runnin' home ice cream in hand
I'd take a walk among the fireflies
But I'm far too drunk to stand

And the plains stretch away in the fading light
In the land of cornfields and the cow
I know that one day I'll be leaving here
Though it's hard to imagine that now…

The sun is gone now, in this Midwestern town
The golf course is dotted with lovers
A Chevrolet goes by with blood in its eye
As daughters go bad like their mothers

And the plains stretch away in the fading light
In the land of cornfields and the cow
I know that one day I'll be leaving here
Though it's hard to imagine that now…

It's such a long way from anywhere
Such a long way to go
I've got a fast car,
But my mind… rolls so slow

And the plains stretch away in the fading light
In the land of cornfields and the cow
I know that one day I'll be leaving here
But I just don't know how
Don't know how

The Dakota Territory

When the wind blows 'cross the prairie
It comes from a thousand miles
Sometimes it comes like a dancer
In the Spring you could say it smiles

But when Winter rules the prairie
The wind blows fire and ice
You could call it a thousand things
Not one of them would be nice
Not one… would be nice

When Spring comes back to the prairie
The rivers crack and roar
The green wipes away the memory
Of the cold wind's rush at the door

The growing time is upon us
The dyin' time fades away
The young 'uns think sun is forever
The elders know only cold can stay
They know…only cold can stay

There's a sod house out on the prairie
The last one across the river
The prairie wind let them drive their stakes
But the wind was an Indian giver

When the blizzard hit last April
They had already eaten their seed
The livestock froze and the baby died
All they could do was plead
Yes all…they could do was plead

Holy

Swing low, Mary Lou
Swing low and easy
Can't no devil get next to you
Swing low and easy

Down through the hills in the valley low
Where life flows easy and the river runs slow
There's an old country woman just off the main road
Who loves God's children just to lighten her load

She's holy
So holy she glows
Good as the North Dakota soil
Strong as the wheat that grows
She's lived one life, got another to go
You know she believes 'cause she says so

She sees sweet Jesus hovering in the sky
He's getting bigger and bigger in her mind's eye
There's a band of angels singing in her ear
To keep her body healthy and her spirit clear

She's holy
So holy she glows
Good as the North Dakota soil
Strong as the wheat that grows
She's lived one life, got another to go
You know she believes because she says so

Swing low, Mary Lou
Swing low and easy
Can't no devil get next to you
Swing low and easy

Gas It Up

Gas it up
Rev up the V-8
The boys are down at the corner
We gonna be out late

Gas it up
Check those tires
Gotta get rollin'
Try to put out the fire

The dirty snow has melted
The river's runnin' high
I got to hit a hundred
A few times before I die

Gas it up
Rev up the V-8
The boys are down at the corner
We gonna be out late

Gas it up
Check those tires
Gotta get rollin'
Try to put out the fire

The girls have got the top down
Stopped and laughin' at the red light
I can feel that motor runnin'
Underneath the hood tonight

Gas it up
Rev up the V-8
The boys are down at the corner
We gonna be out late

Gas it up
Check those tires
Gotta get rollin'
Try to put out the fire

A Question of Style

There's a boy down by the river
Catchin' catfish in the shade
He's too young to care about
The mistakes he has made

Hot dust arisin'
From the road along the shore
You got to eat the apple first
To find the core

The Mississippi River is wide
It takes its sweet time to decide
To roll on, or to stop here for a while

'Cause some things have got to be
It's gonna make it to the sea
The rest is just a question of style

Trucks up on the highway
Rollin' across the plain
Full of destinations
Full of oil and sacks of grain

They roll across the bridge up above
Where the Mississippi flows
They think they're leavin' her behind
But the river knows, yes she does

The Mississippi River is wide
It takes its sweet time to decide
To roll on, or to stop here for a while

'Cause some things have got to be
It's gonna make it to the sea
The rest is just a question of style

My mama's son and your daddy's daughter
Are like Mississippi mud and Mississipi water, uh-huh

Now the boy's sippin' Coca-Cola
Waitin' for the fish to bite
He's not worried 'bout the time
'Cause he's fishin' right

The Mississippi River is wide
It takes its sweet time to decide
To roll on, or to stop here for a while

'Cause some things have got to be
It's gonna make it to the sea
The rest is just a question of style

Black Earth

Just past the junction
Of County 9 and 53
There's a few dusty memories
Where people used to be

A church with no steeple,
School with no bell
The small town of Black Earth
Ain't doin' so well.

The new highway missed it,
Big farms came in.
Young sons and daughters
Started leavin' their kin.

Saturday night they went
To Bismark to dance
The grange had no jukebox
Didn't stand a chance

Black Earth's just a bump in the road
It ain't enough to even shift your load
If you try to find it
I'll tell you straight from the start
Black Earth may be just a place in my heart

It's got no fire station
There's nothing left to burn
But Fred still wears his helmet
He's a little slow to learn

The Johnsons left town
Couldn't make that store run
Elmer blew his brains out
With a 44 gun.

Black Earth's just a bump in the road
It ain't enough to even shift your load
If you try to find it
I'll tell you straight from the start
Black Earth may be just a place in my heart

The sun sets on the prairie
Beer sign goes on
Fred pumps twenty gallons
And he sings a country song

For every truck that stops
There's fifty goes right through
Fred says, "That's the way it is.
What's a man to do?"

Black Earth's just a bump in the road
It ain't enough to even shift your load
If you try to find it
I'll tell you straight from the start
Black Earth may be just a place in my heart

This whole world's my lover

 # The World Rolls On

Some people roll outta bed and curse the mornin'
Some people jump right up and praise the day
Some people choke on their daily bread
They don't know that happy is in your head
If you can't keep movin' you got to get on outta the way

'Cause this world rolls on like a bowlin' ball
Spinnin' softly through space
The stars shine brightly above us all
Gravity keeps us in our place

Young people think that they gonna live on forever
Old people know that they might just die today
Young people hopin' that love is real
Old people tell 'em it's a lousy deal
But young people can't hear a word that old people say

But this world rolls on like a bowlin' ball
Spinnin' softly through space
The stars shine brightly above us all
Gravity keeps us in our place

Poor people livin' in a trailer down by the river
Rich people livin' in a house up on the hill
They got capital gains growin' year to year
Broker on the phone talkin' ear to ear
Poor people just hopin' they can work & eat their fill

And this world rolls on like a bowlin' ball
Spinnin' softly through space
The stars shine brightly above us all
Gravity keeps us in our place

Mama said Boy, you'll never be good for nothin'
Papa said Son, one day you'll do well
Mama said Boy, your butt's too hard
Get out the house now and mow the yard
Papa could be right but it's way too soon to tell

And this world rolls on like a bowlin' ball
Spinnin' softly through space
The stars shine brightly above us all
Gravity keeps us in our place

What That Means

I gotta whole lotta black-eyed peas
And I got me some collard greens
Gonna put 'em with some shoulder pork
And find out what that means
What that means
What that means

Cookin' in the kitchen
Talkin' 'round the oven
Drinkin' one more glass of wine
Dreamin' 'bout our lovin'

Gotta whole lotta memories
I keep 'em in a big ol' jar
Some are sweet as honey
And some they pull me down so far
Down so far

Cookin' in the kitchen
Talkin' 'round the oven
Drinkin' one more glass of wine
Dreamin' 'bout our lovin'

Step out on the porch
If you can't stand the heat
But we won't let it burn us up
We'll let it simmer 'til it's sweet

Took all of my black-eyed peas
My pork and my collard greens
Put in a lovin' spoonful
And I found out what that means
What that means
What that means

Cookin' in the kitchen
Talkin' 'round the oven
Drinkin' one more glass of wine
Dreamin' 'bout our lovin'
Dreamin' 'bout our lovin'

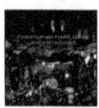

Railway Track

I'm a like a locomotive on a railway track
Rollin' out to the horizon and I don't look back
Put your ear down on the iron you can hear me sing
A-puffin' and a-hummin' it's the same damn thing

Whoo-ooh!   Whoo-ooh!

You might-a seen me chuggin' you won't see me swerve
I'm not a-chasin' my own tail out on Dead Man's Curve
Ain't no room for hesitation on the Pittsburgh line
Cause the coal train is a-comin' and it's right on time

Whoo-ooh!   Whoo-ooh!

I'm feelin all right, not a-feelin no pain
'cause I'm a-drivin, not just a-riding this train

I'm a like a locomotive on a railway track
Rollin' back from the horizon with my clickety-clack
Put your ear down on the iron you can hear me moan
Like my honey in the feathers when I get back home

Whoo-ooh!   Whoo-ooh!

I'm feelin all right, not a-feelin no pain
'cause I'm a-drivin, not just a-riding this train

Whoo- ooh!   Whoo-ooh!

Best I Got

If you're lonely
I'll be your best friend
If you're lonely
I'll be your best friend
Call my number
I'll come 'round again

If you're hungry
I'll make somethin' hot
If you're hungry
I'll make somethin' hot
It may not be that special
But it'll be the best I got

Seems like yesterday is hangin' around
Makin' trouble in the 'hood
I would really love to make a new start
But every time I try it's no good

If you're broken
I'll help you get well
If you're broken
I'll help you get well
If they ask me
I won't ever tell

When I'm lonely
And even when I'm not
When I'm lonely
And even when I'm not
Can I call your number?
'Cause you're the best I got

Can I call your number?
'Cause you're the best I got
The best I got
The best I got
The best I got

High

I can get high
When the wind picks up
And the thunder rolls
On the horizon

I can get high
When the first drops fall
And I know that the river
Will soon be risin'

But she's steppin' toward the rainbow
There's somethin' in her style
I mostly get high
On my baby's smile

I can get high
On a glass of wine in the kitchen
When friend I believe in
Is telling our story

I can get high
When I realize
That what we have right now
Is better than old glory

But at the kitchen table
When I've been gone for a while
I mostly get high
On my baby's smile.

I was blinded by the glitter
But things are simpler now
Those who were working backstage
Have come out for a bow

I can get high
When one of my boys is around
And I know that he's doin'
The best that he can

I can get high
On the future now
'Cause I've seen my own child
Become a man

But she's a mother and a lover
She's gone the extra mile
I mostly get high
On my baby's smile

Hockey Éternité

Music : Christopher Mark Jones
Words : Bernard Pozier and Christopher Mark Jones

C'est un enfant qui joue dans la ruelle
Mille et mille fois il lance la rondelle
Dans un filet de hockey imaginaire
Il lance et compte en supplémentaire

A son âge il a tout son temps
Il joue chaque jour avec les autres enfants
Et déjoue déjà les plus vieux
Avec ses bras levés aux cieux

Dans une ligue semi-professionnelle
Mille et mille fois il lance la rondelle
Il rêve toujours année après année
De soulever enfin sa coupe Stanley

Dans la force de l'âge il oublie le temps
C'est une star dans le regard des enfants
Il vit l'illusion de ne jamais être vieux
Il traverse la glace les bras levés aux cieux

Dans chaque lancer chaque coup de patin
Il y a le rêve il y a l'instinct
Plaisir et désir emmêlés
Et dans la bouche un goût d'éternité

Dans l'aréna de son arrondissement
Il joue encore malgré le poids des ans
Avec ses amis en fin de soirée
Il rêve encore au divin trophée

Il n'a pas d'âge il n'y a pas de temps
Son corps est en déclin mais son cœur est constant
Adulte enfant et déjà un peu vieux
Avec toujours les bras levés aux cieux
Avec toujours les bras levés aux cieux

Hockey Eternity [Hockey Éternité]

Music : Christopher Mark Jones
Words : Bernard Pozier and Christopher Mark Jones

There's a child playing in the alley
Thousands of times he shoots the puck
Into an imaginary hockey net
He shoots and scores in overtime

At his age he has time aplenty
He plays every day with the other children
And already outplays his elders
With his arms raised to the sky

In a semi-professional league
Thousands of times he shoots the puck
He still dreams year after year
Of finally lifting his own Stanley Cup

In the prime of his life he forgets time
He's a star in the eyes of the children
He lives the illusion of never growing old
Crossing the ice with his arms raised to the sky

In each shot each push of a skate
There is the dream and there is instinct
Pleasure and desire mixed together
And in his mouth a taste of eternity

In his neighborhood skating rink
He still plays despite his advancing years
With his friends at evening's end
He still dreams of the divine trophy

He's without age, time doesn't exist
His body is in decline but his heart is constant
Child adult and already getting old
With his arms still raised to the sky

Whatever you do

Whatever you do
Keep a hand on the wheel
And an eye on the road
It's the only way to get home
With a heavy load

Whatever you do
Keep a peaceful mind
Then neither good luck nor bad
Will catch you from behind

I looked out my window last night
And the stars you know
They were shining so bright
They were all lined up
To see you through
Whatever you do
Whatever you do

Whatever I do
I'll take my time about it
If it's too much for me
I can do without it

Whatever I do
I won't be afraid to climb
nor afraid to fall
Sometimes you know
It's the loser who takes all
I looked out the window today
And all four winds they were blowin' my way
To fill my sails
And see me through
Whatever I do
Whatever I do

Whatever we do
Let's try to keep in mind
What we've been through so far
We've helped each other
Be who we are

Whatever we do
Let's keep a part of the fool
And a part of the clown
It'll make us stronger if we lay our burden down
From time to time

Tonight out my window
I don't see a thing
But deep inside
You know it feels like spring
And that's all we need
To see us through
Whatever we do
Whatever we do

That's all we need
To see us through

Don't Look Behind

In the misty morning
The splash of paddles on the lake
A father, son and walleyes
Head to head

I asked Dad, do you regret
The decisions that you made?
He smiled at my question
Then he said

Don't look behind
Just clear your mind
Your path will rise before you
Like a highway line
Don't look behind

Now many other mornings
Have come and moved along
And some blue skies have changed
To thunder cloud

And when at times I've wondered
If I could face the dawn
I have found myself repeating
Right out loud

Don't look behind
Just clear your mind
Your path will rise before you
Like a highway line
Don't look behind

The wind may blow from east or west
Just let it fill your sails
Sometimes the least advice is best
Don't look behind

Another misty morning
The splash of paddles on the lake
Another father, son and walleyes
Head to head

The boy asked Dad do you regret
The decisions that you made?
I laughed at his question
Then I said

Don't look behind
Just clear your mind
Don't look behind
Just clear your mind
Your path will rise before you
Like a highway line
Don't look behind

 # Cincinnati Night

The smog's sittin' heavy
On the Ohio river
Night sky lit up
Like an old cabaret

Out on the porch
Leanin' back in the shadows
There's two tired angels
With a lot less to say

This whole world's my lover
Gonna squeeze her real tight
On a Cincinnati night

Only been here a day
But brothers and sisters
Make you feel like a window
Washed and seen through

A lone country fiddle
Cryin' out from the kitchen
It's so good when nothin'
Is the right thing to do

This whole world's my lover
Gonna squeeze her real tight
On a Cincinnati night

There's good years before me
And good years behind
And don't your lovin' flow easy
When you got your peace of mind

Spaced out on the highway
I'm a Greyhound believer
Dayton and Pittsburgh
Left down the track

I dream Cincinnati
Lyin dreamless behind me
And I hear the night laughter
Callin' me back

This whole world's my lover
Gonna squeeze her real tight
On a Cincinnati night

Walkin' 19

Walkin' 19 with my headphones on
Listening to Brownie McGhee
Thinking that the time has come and gone
When a man could oughta be so free
I hum a tune out on the evening breeze
And hope it comes back to me

Kickin' cobblestones on an Oslo street
Meditatin' *dans le noir*
Wonderin' how it all has come to this
Wonderin' how we got so far
Come Shine rippin' the standards up
Groovin' in Herr Nilsen's bar

Catching my piece of the music
Hoping I can play in time
Not too hard to tell it's gonna turn out well
As long as I can stay in rhyme
Stay in rhyme

Walkin' with my honey out on rue Mouffetard
She tells me not to hold too tight
That *petit steak-frites* and that *Côtes du Rhône*
Sure can make you feel just right
We walk straight down the rue St. Jacques
Into that Paris night

Walkin' 19 with my headphones on
Listening to Brownie McGhee
Thinking that the time is still goin' on
And I can still be so free
I hum a tune out on the evening breeze
It always comes back to me

The sweet sound of lawnmowers

 **Mrs. Pennington**

They moved from the city
She left all her friends
But they had the money
And it seemed to make sense

There was no point in working
Lawyers did well
Now it's too late to start
She wouldn't know what to sell

Mrs. Pennington sits by the window
Faded photographs spread on the chair
Where her husband would sleep,
Before he went away
Mrs. Pennington doesn't know where

The children came quickly
She drove them to school
They had swimming lessons
She sat by the pool

Now they're off to college
Empty rooms down the hall
A few days at Christmas
And they rarely call

Mrs. Pennington sits by the window
Faded photographs spread on the chair
Where her husband would sleep,
Before he went away
Mrs. Pennington doesn't know where

What once was a dream
Has turned into a cage
And like her Polaroid pictures
Has faded with age

Mrs. Pennington ponders
How to find her way back
From this great shuttered house
On a dark cul-de-sac

Where the cats scream at night
And the memories crowd
And the sounds of her silence
Are crying out loud

Mrs. Pennington sits by the window
Faded photographs spread on the chair
Where her husband would sleep,
Before he went away
Mrs. Pennington doesn't know where
Nor if he found what he was looking for
There

Drivin'

I'm gonna keep on drivin'
Keep drivin' on
I'm gonna keep on drivin'
Til the road is gone
I got an achin' inside me
No one to guide me
So I'll keep on driving
Keep drivin' on

Got up last Monday
Put on my shoes
Thought of my working day
Got the working day blues

Got in my car
Heard the big engine's roar
Remembered that drivin'
Is what I'm workin' for

I'm gonna keep on drivin'
Keep drivin' on
I'm gonna keep on drivin'
Til the road is gone
They'll never find me
I'll leave 'em all behind me
I'll keep on drivin'
Keep drivin' on

I hated high school
Wanted to party and drive
Took the first job goin'
That would keep me alive

My Lisa likes ridin'
I pick her up at school
Her college friends can't believe it
They think I'm a fool

I'm gonna keep on drivin'
Keep drivin' on
I'm gonna keep on drivin'
Til the road is gone
Life's full of red lights
You can get lost in the headlights
But I keep on drivin'
Keep drivin' on

Came home last Monday
Swung 'round the block
Walked up the steps
Put the key in the lock

The house was in darkness
A note on the door
Now I got nothing
To be comin' home for

I'll just keep on drivin'
Keep drivin' on
I'm gonna keep on drivin'
Til the road is gone
I got no one to love me
She thinks she's above me
So I'll keep on drivin'
Keep drivin' on
Keep drivin' on
Keep drivin' on.

Home At Last

This ain't LA
And it ain't no Paris France
But it could be nice
If we give it half a chance

There's trees along the back yard
Good neighbors down the street
We'll have room for children
Life could be so sweet

Home at last
Home at last
Baby I think we're home at last

This job I think will keep me
You can find work too
We'll plant ourselves a garden
Our roamin' days are through

I'll stay away from barrooms
Stop my wanderin' eye
I swear you've seen the last time
The last time I make you cry

Home at last
Home at last
Baby I think we're home at last

I've been livin' like a train wreck
Goin' too fast for the station
I know you want to get off
But it's a whole new situation

This ain't LA
And it ain't no Paris France
But it could be nice

If we give it half a chance
There's trees along the back yard
Good neighbors down the street
We'll have room for children
Life could be so sweet

Home at last
Home at last
Baby I think we're home at last

Home at last
Home at last
Baby I hope we're home ...
At last

 **Suburban Two-Step**

On any given Sunday
I can roll out of bed
The sweet sound of lawnmowers
Echoing through my head

Which means that fathers and sons
Are out there doin' the deeds
That come with having more land
Than any one family needs

Mom's at the market
Buyin' sausage and cheese
Sis is in the basement
She's down on her knees

'Cause Billy slept over
He was too drunk to drive
In a miracle of nature
He's come back to life

Suburban two-step
On the right side of the tracks
One step up one step back

We'll get back together
When the churches let out
The flat screens will light up
And you'll hear people shout

At games played by big men
Many larger than life
They got that way with needles
And domestic strife

Someone's called out for pizza
Heather's gone off her meds
We're up by three touchdowns
At least in her head

When the last whistle blows
The lawnmowers start up again
The grills are all smoking
Say Billy where have you been?

Suburban two-step
On the right side of the tracks
One step up one step back

Dusk settles on the backyards
In this Technicolor dream
Eminem goes by on a car radio
I hear my neighbors scream

The bricks have all been pointed
The lawn is Chemlawn fine
Sis is back from rehab
But Momma's back on the wine

Pappa's in his man room
With a whisky and cigar
He can't wait til Monday
To get back in his car

The pressure of perfection
Is more than he can stand
Looking 'round the table
Seems like we've played our last hand

Suburban two-step
On the right side of the tracks
One step up one step back
One step up two steps back

The sweet sound of lawnmowers

I saw the sea come slowly rising

Lordstown

Grandpa tired of farming
Of working 14 hours a day
So he signed on at Lordstown
To build the Chevrolet

He bought himself a ranch house
In a suburb north of town
And watched TV on Sunday
The Cleveland Indians and the Browns

He drove up to Lordstown
Parked his Chevy in the lot
And thanked God for the paycheck
Every time he punched the clock
Every time he punched the clock

Daddy was a prom king
He was Grandpa's favored son
He spent too much time on football
While his schoolwork went undone

Yes Daddy was a fullback
On the high school team
But a knee twist at the goal line
Blew up his college dream

So he drove up to Lordstown
Parked his Chevy in the lot
And thanked God for the paycheck
Every time he punched the clock
Every time he punched the clock

I went off to college
And I'm proud of what I know
But the jobs that I've been offered
Won't pay off what I owe

Between the layoffs and the robots
I won't get what Daddy had
But at least I'm working
And Jesus, am I glad

So I drive up to Lordstown,
I park my Chevy in the lot
And I thank God for the paycheck
Every time I punch the clock
Every time I punch the clock

Big Mac

Until I get home
Leave the shades down
Don't want those gangsters
To know you're around
Don't answer the phone
Until I get back
I've got some money
We can share a Big Mac

No that's not your daddy
Daddy won't be home soon
He looks out through the bars
And howls at the moon
Daddy did what he had to
Or that's what he thought
The money was fine
Until he got caught

Oh Lord my Lord
He was running wild
Oh Lord please Lord
Not my child

Don't sit out on the porch
That's where Bobby went down
Those clowns in the alley
Just messin' around

Do what I say
Don't do what I do
I'm out here on the street
Don't let it be you

*Oh Lord my Lord
I'm running wild
Oh Lord please Lord
Not my child*

*Oh Lord my Lord
I'm running wild
Oh Lord please Lord
Save my child*

Until I get home
Leave the shades down
Don't want those gangsters
To know you're around

Don't answer the phone
Until I get back
I've got some money
We can share a Big Mac
Share a Big Mac
Share a Big Mac

Steelhead Blues

Agnes Horne likes to peck and swoon
She lives on tea and chitchat
She was born with a silver spoon
And she can't seem to forget that

Her lovin' friends tried to make her change
But she didn't wanna know
The slightest bend made her feel strange
And she was afraid that it might show

She's got the steelhead blues
He's got lead in his shoes
She's been living in the past
Just prayin' it's gonna last
She's got the steelhead blues

Uncle Jim is an oilman
He knows how the country cooks
Life to him is his oilcans
And his double sets of books

He thinks things are outta hand
With these niggers runnin' wild
So he sings This Land is My Land
And he strokes his only child

He's got the steelhead blues
He's got lead in his shoes
He's been living in the past
Just prayin' it's gonna last
He's got the steelhead blues

Now them steelhead blues is bad blues
And those leaden shoes is heavy
The storm that's comin' is a bad storm
So we might as well get ready

When the brothers take your number
They're not likely to be nice
When they ask which side you stand on
They're not gonna ask you twice

You've got the steelhead blues
You've got lead in your shoes
You've been living in the past
Just prayin' it's gonna last
You've got the steelhead blues

But you should know by now
I can't believe that nobody told you
That it can't last
It can't last

All They Seek

She walked out of love
Like you get up from a chair
Just slammed the door
And left him standing there
She was too tired
Of swimming upstream

She didn't turn back,
Not a second look
She knew the ending
She had read the book
And he found out
It was not just a bad dream

Sometimes the weak will be strong
Sometimes the strong will be weak
Sometimes the right will be wrong
And lose all they seek
Lose all they seek

He was the people's choice
He had all the votes
A rising tide
Lifted all his boats
The faithful sat behind him
Smiling on stage

Then the same old dogs
Chewin' the same old bone
Took all the money
Hung up the telephone
His hopes turned grey
Well before his age

Sometimes the weak will be strong
Sometimes the strong will be weak
Sometimes the right will be wrong
And lose all they seek
Lose all they seek

He burned the bacon
And he broke the yolks
His new religion
Was just a joke
He was slipping off
Of the saints' parade

All his buddies
Were the lonely ones
They talked through bourbon
And they stroked their guns.
They played their manhood
Like a sad charade

Sometimes the weak will be strong
Sometimes the strong will be weak
Sometimes the right will be wrong
And lose all they seek
All they seek

I saw the sea come slowly rising

The Blackstone Rangers

I lived in a low small house
Down across the tracks
With a broke-down truck
By the tool shed 'round the back

My Daddy loaded flat cars
Down near the state line
On a Saturday night
He drank that clear moonshine

But when the Blackstone Rangers
Came to town
Right then I knew
They couldn't keep us down
Couldn't keep us down

I was a dark-skinned boy
In a light-skinned place
The African sun
Written on my face

Momma said it ain't that different
From our place down South
But you'll be all right
If you can watch your mouth

When the Blackstone Rangers
Came to town
Then I knew
They couldn't keep us down
Couldn't keep us down

Six big men
Ridin' six big bikes
Rollin' down my street
Cool as you like

Just then the bright sun
Went back under a cloud
I heard a woman cry out
Heard her cry out loud

My cousin Leroy
He made a bad choice
Went down to Chicago
Where they heard his voice

When he couldn't find the money
For the deal he made
The Rangers shined the light
He couldn't find the shade

The Blackstone Rangers
Came to town
And Leroy knew
He shouldn't be around

The Blackstone Rangers
Came to town
They put him underground

 **Roseland**

It's a cool wet night down in Soho
The whores are all in off the street
Just a few lonely cruisers, a few three-time losers
Are out with the cops on the beat

Some of the boys at the Circus
Are feeling like they're in too deep
One or two strippers are headin' home for their kippers
The light'll come before they sleep

Meanwhile out here in Roseland
Everybody knows they've been had
They just don't know how bad

In Chinatown the lights are still flashin'
As the black night starts turnin' gray
A stray dog gets a sweet and sour breakfast
But down here they don't call him a stray

The big-time hustlers are leavin'
While the pimps and the junkies talk jive
And the Queen of them all down at the end of the Mall
She don't even know they're alive

Meanwhile out here in Roseland
Everybody knows they've been had
They just don't know how bad

In Roseland alarm clocks go crazy
They roll out of bed into line
They sneak into town on the Underground
Thinkin' "Everything's all right, I've got mine."

They'd like to go down to Djibouti
But they'd have to give up the kids and the car
They like the bright lights and the bargain flights
But they'd never take it that far.

Meanwhile out here in Roseland
Everybody knows they've been had
They just don't know how bad

Meanwhile out here in Roseland
Out here in Roseland
Everybody knows they've been had
And they're oh so glad…

Miguel y Celestina

I answered the door
It was my neighbor John
With a petition
He asked me to sign

He said all the illegals
Were getting him down
And it was high time
That we drew the line

Now John is my neighbor
And I call him my friend
But he's not makin' ends meet
No more

He was angry at people
That he thought were strangers
So I asked him to
Look right next door

What of Miguel y Celestina
Y su hija Maria Isabel
We can't let this anger come between us
If we just stand together
We'll all do well

Miguel worked the orchards
From Texas to Maine
Lived in ramshackle barracks
Worked in heat and in rain

He sent for Celestina
Then Maria was born
A Midwestern Mexicana
Raised on chiles and corn

So I'll stand by Miguel y Celestina
Y su hija Maria Isabel
I won't let this anger come between us
If we stand together
We'll all do well

My people were northern
They came here in ships

There were many who died on the way
They loved where they came from
But had nothing to lose
It's not all that different today

So let's stand by Miguel y Celestina
Y su hija Maria Isabel
We can't let this anger come between us
If we stand together
We'll all do well

Hoop dreams

I got a good left hand
I can take it to the hole
Got the rainbow jumper
And the finger roll
Ain't that big
But my first step is quick
Got the nice jump stop
My step-through is slick
The college girls know
I'm the next big thing
Angie ain't shy
About showin' my ring

Hoop dreams
They're drivin' me crazy
Keepin' me up at night
Hoop dreams
You know I'm not lazy
I'm just keepin' my dreams in sight
Hoop dreams
Hoop dreams

When I broke my foot
The coach wouldn't listen
I told him six weeks
Was all I'd be missin'
And that weed they found on me
At that party at Dan's
My so-called friends
They dropped it and ran
It looks bad in the paper
I was on a full ride
From what I been hearin'
I'll be on the outside

Hoop dreams
They're drivin me crazy
Keepin' me up at night
Hoop dreams
You know I'm not lazy
I'm just keepin' my dreams in sight
Hoop dreams

There's glass on the asphalt
In this rusty old town
All the rims are danglin'.
The backboards are fallin' down

Back in my home town
I'm pumpin' gas
Waitin' for Christmas
Sittin' on my ass
In the city leagues
I'm a big name
Ain't nobody here
Has got my game
But I put on some weight
It's got me to thinkin'
If I want another shot
I'm gonna have to stop drinkin'

Hoop dreams
They're drivin' me crazy
Keepin' me up at night
Hoop dreams
You know I'm not lazy
I'm just keepin' my dreams in sight
Hoop dreams
Hoop dreams

Dans la ville

J'suis venu dans la ville
Y avait plus rien à la campagne
J'ai tant et tant perdu
Il fallait bien qu'je gagne
Quelques maudites pièces
Pour chauffer mes fesses
Dans la ville

Ma pauv' mère est morte
À son dixième enfant
On n'est pas plus heureux
D'être des vivants
Dans cette basse misère
Qui écrase même la prière
Dans la ville
Dans la ville

J'ai même pas eu le temps
De pleurer ma vieille
Y a peut-être encore du bonheur
Au fond de cette bouteille

Mes frères sont tous partis
Partis pour les États
J' ai pus rien entendu
Ils m'écrivent pas
Y savent non plus où j'habite
Et que j'ai perdu ma petite
Dans la ville
Dans la ville

Faudrait d'abord que je m'endorme
Avant de penser au réveil
Mais 'y a peut-être encore du bonheur
Au fond de cette bouteille

Je vis dans la ville
Y a pus rien à la campagne
J'ai tant et tant perdu
Il faut bien qu'je gagne
Quelques maudites pièces
Pour chauffer mes fesses
Dans la ville
Dans la ville
Dans la ville

In The City [Dans la ville]

I came to the city
There was nothing left in the country
I've lost so much
I had no choice but to earn
A few lousy bucks
To keep my butt warm
In the city

My poor mother died
Giving birth to her tenth child
We're no better off
To be among the living
In this lowdown misery
That crushes even prayer
In the city

I never even had time
To cry for my old lady
There might still be some happiness
At the bottom of this bottle

My siblings all took off
Took off for the States
I've never heard a word
They don't write
And they don't know where I live anyway
And that I lost my little one
In the city

First I need to get some sleep
Before I can think of waking
But there may still be some happiness
At the bottom of this bottle

I live in the city
There's nothing left in the country
I've lost so much
Somehow I have to earn
A few lousy bucks
To keep my butt warm
In the city
In the city
In the city

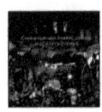

I Saw the Sea Come Slowly Rising

I saw the sea come slowly rising
While the white glaciers slipped away
I saw the seasons shift
And the migrations drift
While profits kept on growing day to day

I saw the butterflies bewildered
As the oil rigs pierced the ground
I saw the land
Pass from hand to hand
I heard the farmers' grieving sound

Now is the time
To put names to these crimes
To gather your friends and mine
And draw the line

I saw the guns in every hand
And the child soldiers that were hired
I saw the blood
In a crimson flood
In the names of many gods the shots were fired

I saw the faceless corporations
Hiding behind policemen's shields
I saw the mothers' fears
Turn to mothers' tears
I saw the fresh graves in the fields

Now is the time
To put names to these crimes
To gather your friends and mine
And draw the line

Behind our television fantasies
The masters of the universe preside
The theft of nature's bounty by a self-chosen few
Will with the thirst for bread and justice soon collide

I saw the newspapers defeated
And their great voices slowly fade
I saw the poets' bark
Turn to whispers in the dark
While the information oligarchs got paid

I saw the voters turned away
By rules that we had seen before
Jim Crow in the night
Protecting all that's white
As money bought elections by the score

Now is the time
To put names to these crimes
To gather your friends and mine
And draw the line

You spoke to me with fingertips

Spoken For

Wandering in the summer green
When things may not be as they seem
She was pretty so was he
They talked of lands beyond the sea
Then she said Do not misinterpret what this means

'Cause I'm spoken for
Yes I'm spoken for
There's a little less glitter
But a lot more gold
And he will love me when I'm old
I'm spoken for
Spoken for

He was where he might have stayed
But he knew she had only strayed
When she touched his chest and raised her brow
He said I cannot allow
To let you throw your one best chance away

'Cause you're spoken for
I know you're spoken for
There's a little less glitter
But a lot more gold
And you'll still love him when you're old
You're spoken for
Spoken for

And the carousel goes round
To the organ's circus sound
When it stops will you know how
To put your feet back on the ground?

Now I look across the bed
And wonder at the things we've said
And every day we've fought & won
The right to be not two but one
The words remembered echo in my head

'Cause now I'm spoken for
Yes I'm spoken for
There's a little less glitter
A lot more gold
And I'll still love you when we're old
I'm spoken for
Yes, I'm spoken for
Spoken for

Love's not a fashion

Love's not a fashion
You can learn from a magazine
It's not the bells nor the cymbals crashin'
It's how you feel in the days in between

When morning came she didn't look like an angel
Her hair was black down at the roots
Could not remember what I was after
So I went after my boots

At the bedside the devil was waiting
I should have known he would have to be paid
Why can't it be simple
For a man to love a maid

Love's not a fashion
You can learn from a magazine
It's not the bells nor the cymbals crashin'
It's how you feel in the days in between

I wonder what happened to Nancy
That Polish girl from the Midwest
Of all my teenage visions
I could see her the best

But she went up to Milwaukee
And I moved out to the coast
Now sometimes I dream without knowing
And she comes like a beautiful ghost

Yes I know that
Love's not a fashion
You can learn from a magazine
It's not the bells nor the cymbals crashin'
It's how you feel in the days in between

Now love can't be bought on Wall Street
It don't come with a guarantee
You can have it but you can't hold it
Just let it be

Yes I know that
Love's not a fashion
You can learn from a magazine
It's not the bells nor the cymbals crashin'
It's how you feel in the days in between

Yes

Walkin' along with my baby
In the moonlight
Shinin' through the big oak trees
In the park

Fireflies blinkin' around us
In the warm night
Brushin' her arm I could feel it
Feel the spark

*I whispered into the darkness
Can I kiss you ?
She said Yes, Yes, Yes.*

Standin' so still with my baby
In the moonlight
Shinin' through the big oak trees
On her face

The night was holdin' its breath
All around us
We had come a thousand years
To this place

*I whispered into the darkness
Can I touch you?
She said Yes, Yes, Yes*

Lyin' so still with my baby
In the moonlight
Shinin' through the big oak trees
All around

We were sharin' our breath
In the warm night
Almost afraid to believe
What we'd found

I whispered into the darkness
Will you keep me?
She said Yes, Yes, Yes
Yes, Yes, Yes

I'll Stay By Your Side

I'll stay by your side
Stay by your side
To care and abide
I'll stay by your side

Way out on the horizon
The sky meets the land
But distance and solitude
Disappear where we stand
And all of our journey
In the touch of your hand

I'll stay by your side
Stay by your side
To care and abide
I'll stay by your side

I can hear my own heartbeat
In the house of my fears
The wind shakes the windows
But we're warm in here
There's no smoke and no mirrors
My mind has never been so clear

I'll stay by your side
Stay by your side
To care and abide
I'll stay by your side

So I'll sing our song
Sing it sweet and long
Cause my love's still strong
In my heart

I'll stay by your side
Stay by your side
To care and abide
I'll stay by your side
To care and abide
I'll stay by your side

Muffins

It's six o'clock in the morning
The temperature's thirteen degrees
Jennifer's walking down Main Street
She's still a bit weak in the knees

She opens the door to the bakery
Hangs her coat up and turns on the light
Mixes blueberries into the batter
Fills the muffin tins perfectly right

She heats up the oven and slides in the trays
Then she sees the muffins rise
Like the love light in his eyes

At eight o'clock doors will open
At just about nine he arrives
With his green eyes, his scarf & his mittens
He's a cat full of too many lives

He asks for a blueberry muffin
And kisses her once on the cheek
That's all it takes to remember
The times they had no time to speak

She heats up the oven and slides in the trays
Then she sees the muffins rise
Like the love light in his eyes

One day he comes in at nine-thirty
One day he asks for a scone
He turns left and right,
Ill at ease in the light
Then she notices he's not alone
He's not alone

It's six o'clock in the morning
The temperature's 13 degrees
Jennifer's walking down Main Street
She's still a bit weak in the knees

She opens the door to the bakery
Hangs her coat up and turns on the lights
Mixes blueberries into the batter
Fills the muffin tins perfectly right

She heats up the oven and slides in the trays
When she sees the muffins rise
Her tears are no surprise

Morning Glory

Morning glory
Morning sun
Morning glory
When we'll be one

I've lain with many women
Touched many a pretty face
But there ain't any woman
Can take your place

Walkin' down the highway
Your memory in my pack
I can only hope you'll be there
When I get back

Morning glory
Morning sun

It's been a long love's season
We've had our winters and our springs
But I can still hear the robin
When he sings

I see your slender body
Your spirit bright as fire
And I tell myself to climb down
Off this wire

Morning glory
Morning sun

Your love is like a fountain
Though I drink, it's ever full
Through the bad dream of our distance
I feel it pull

There'll come a sunny morning
Together when we're whole
Just thinking of that morning
Frees my soul

Morning glory
Morning sun
Morning glory
When we'll be one

Ballerina

Dance, ballerina, dance
Dance, ballerina, dance
Dance 'til your mind is too weary to think,
Then you'll sleep

As a child she was gentle
Too gentle it seems
For the world often hurt her
And twisted her dreams

But as her body grew
She taught it to fly
And in moments of sadness
She never would cry, she'd just

Dance, ballerina, dance
Dance, ballerina, dance
Dance 'til your mind is too weary to think,
Then you'll sleep
Then you'll sleep

She grew straight and strong
Her hair finest gold
Her skin of the softness
That's never been sold

It was just in her eyes
That pain found its nest
One could read there the torment
That would not let her rest, so she'd

Dance, ballerina, dance
Dance, ballerina, dance
Dance 'til your mind is too weary to think,
Then you'll sleep

It so happens I loved her
Loved wild and strong
And though she came gladly
She could not stay long

For inside was her hunger
And the hungry aren't free
And oft when beside me
Was where she should be, she would

Dance, ballerina, dance
Dance, ballerina, dance
Dance 'til your mind is too weary to think,
Then you'll sleep

Then one day from a distance
She sent me the news
She was tired and open
She'd hung up her shoes

As I sit here and wonder
If time will be kind
Behind my closed eyelids
In the light of my mind

You still dance
You still dance, ballerina

You still dance, ballerina, dance
Dance, ballerina, dance
Dance 'til your mind is too weary to think,
Then you'll sleep
Then you'll sleep

 # Bobby & Ginnie

Bobby came home from the laundromat
He set down his clothes and his keys
He was alone in his two-room flat
Now he could do what he pleased

'Cause Ginnie had moved back to Memphis
She took both the kid and the car
So Bobby took down her photograph
That hung on the wall like a scar

Ginnie drove off in the Mustang
When Jimbo sat next to their son
She knew even Bobbie would soon divine
That he just could not be the one

Ginnie had loved with abandon
But abandoned was all Bobbie got
Bobbie took down his George T. Stagg
And poured himself a double shot

It was so hard to believe that his business
Had been nothing but foolin' around
Happy was something he'd dreamed of
Lonely was all that he'd found

Bobbie turned on the TV
And watched Geraldo for a while
The people he used to make fun of
Could no longer get him to smile

He thought about making his exit
Of putting a slug in his head
Bobbie took down his 22
And shot up the TV instead

It was so hard to believe that his business
Had been nothing but foolin' around
Happy was something he'd dreamed of
Lonely was all that he'd found

Happy was something he'd dreamed of
Lonely was all that he'd found

Road to Spain

If you want a lovin' man
I'm what you need
You want a garden in your head
I've got the seed
But if you want to settle down
Don't come my way
Though I'll love you like the rising sun
I know I can't stay
Forever is a lonely word
Let's start with today

I met her on a silent mountain
On the road to Spain
Spoke to her of time and highways
She spoke to me of pain
Evening found me satisfied
Laying in her arms
I was broken in her golden skin
Captured by her charms

The days went by like butterflies
Driftin' through the trees
I wrote her name in the sand
Heard it on the breeze
Then she asked me to stay
And I knew I must say
Forever is a lonely word
Let's start with today

If you want a lovin' man
I'm what you need
You want a garden in your head
I've got the seed
But if you want to settle down
Don't come my way
Though I'll love you like the rising sun
I know I can't stay
Forever is a lonely word
Let's start with today

Field of Dreams

You were my new girlfriend
I had my brother's car
We drove out to Turtle Creek
It didn't seem that far

The stream was high and mighty
Spring was in our blood
You spoke to me with fingertips
And words came in a flood

The pasture's edge was blooming
With daisies dressed in green
And when we laid our blanket down
It was our field of dreams
It was our field of dreams

On a midnight highway
Dusted white with snow
Hoping my old car would last
To bring me to your door

We were down and out together
Rich in beggar's clothes
A candle on the table
A bed made on the floor

A draft blew cold around us
Our breath came out like steam
But when we laid our blanket down
It was our field of dreams
It was our field of dreams

Now it's just the two of us
With children on their own
Driving back to Turtle Creek
It feels like going home

The dusk is quiet around us
In late September light
And you hold me softly
There's no need to hold me tight

The harvest tied and bundled
But memories burst through the seams
And when we lay our blanket down
It's still our field of dreams
It's still our field of dreams

The trail of lost and found

The Fire So Soon

He lived on the rotted fruit
From the markets of Marseille
His future never longer
Than the hours of a day

He played his silver whistle
With the gypsies in their camps
Slept beneath the wagons
In the cold and the damp

Songs of forgiveness, chants of the brave,
Hymns of oblivion, of princes & slaves
Body of innocence, soul of the moon,
Smoke on the meadow, the fire so soon

She was dancing with her lover
Across the color line
Said she'd leave South Africa
It was 1969

She asked me for some money
To help pay for her flight
She'd look him up in Memphis
And it would all be right

Songs of forgiveness, chants of the brave,
Hymns of oblivion, of princes & slaves
Body of innocence, soul of the moon,
Smoke on the meadow, the fire so soon

He was working in the barrios
Well-dressed among the tatters
Blessed and believing
He thought that he could matter

When the police came to take him
No one was surprised
His comrades crossed the border
In the dark of the night

Songs of forgiveness, chants of the brave,
Hymns of oblivion, of princes & slaves
Body of innocence, soul of the moon,
Smoke on the meadow, the fire so soon

 **Uncertain Times**

Sometimes I'm runnin' in circles
Others flyin' straight as a shot
One day I have friends aplenty
The next I don't know what I got

Yesterday I was prayin' for prison
Today I want to be freed
These are uncertain times,
Yes, indeed

Those that once were happy
Have soured and grown sad
Those that had a reason
Have squandered what they had
Those that used to help me
Now all come to plead
These are uncertain times, yes indeed

Those that were happily married
They're near all divorced
Once they could dance the night away
They still can, if they're forced
Once they had everything
Now they are in need
These are uncertain times, yes indeed

Sometimes I'm runnin' in circles
Others flyin' straight as a shot
One day I have friends aplenty
The next I don't know what I got

Yesterday I was praying for prison
Today I want to be freed
These are uncertain times,
Yes, indeed

But we're gonna make it through
We're gonna make it through
We're gonna make it through
And I really do hope
That is true

No More Range To Roam

His mother never told him
There were wars to be fought
She got him high on what he could do
Never told him what he could not

He had a crazy dream
He was a cowboy raised on whipped cream
Riding for justice down a dusty trail
On a horse with white paws and a fluffy tail

Little cowboy, get on home
Don't you know there ain't no more range to roam
Little comboy, get on home while you can
There ain't no more range to roam

He hunted salamanders
Climbed in leafy trees
Turned up late for Sunday School
With mud on his knees

His father taught him to be true
He said People remember the good in what you do
It's the White Man's Burden, the Red Man's Law
He was striking a match, hopin' winter would thaw

Little cowboy, get on home
Don't you know there ain't no more range to roam
Little cowboy, get on home while you can
There ain't no more range to roam

Nobody told him
That the young must grow old
That even the strongest love
Must turn cold

So he went on his righteous way
Always knowing the right word to say
And got crushed by a train one windy night
He was moving too fast to see the light

All you cowboys
Get on home while you can
Don't you know there ain't no more range to roam
There ain't no more range…to roam.

 **Autumn Song**

Red autumn leaves
Piled in the yard
Crumpled stories of summer
And working too hard

I feel rise inside me
As the shadows grow long
The sweet and the bitter
Of my autumn song

There'll be one more morning
Or so I believe
And spring will remember
To wake and to breathe

But for now I hum softly
A small song without words
That reminds me of evenings
And the wonders I've heard

There are no more beginnings
The harvest is in
Fires flicker toward darkness
In a whispering wind

What's gone is forever
What was pleasure is pain
We pray for forgiveness
In the cold autumn rain

There'll be one more morning
Or so I believe
And spring will remember
To wake and to breathe

But for now I hum softly
A small song without words
That reminds me of evenings
And the wonders I've heard

 # I Work Hard for a Livin'

It ain't never been easy
I been mostly on my own
Life on a shoestring
Is all I've ever known

There was a time in Tennessee
When I thought I'd lose my mind
'Cause husbands, you know they come and go
But the children stay behind

I work hard for a livin'
I pay for my dreams
I know just what is crazy
And what is as it seems

When I kiss my children
And go out on the town
When you pass by my table
You won't see a frown

My old house is drafty
My Chevy's 'bout to quit
My little girl needs braces
My boy's coat don't fit

But I got no regrets
About being back on my own
Jimmy was a drinker
And he was mean when he came home

I work hard for a livin'
I pay for my dreams
I know just what is crazy
And what is as it seems

When I kiss my children
And go out on the town
When you pass by my table
You won't see a frown

You might say I'm older
I won't say that I'm wise
I don't climb no more mountains
I just cut 'em down to size

There ain't as many friends around me
But them that are should be
And when they hug me tight
Is when I feel like I'm free

I work hard for a livin'
I pay for my dreams
I know just what is crazy
And what is as it seems

When I kiss my children
And go out on the town
When you pass by my table
You won't see a frown

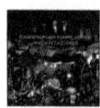
Incantations

I was born among believers
In the green & dripping West
Read Kerouac's new Bible
And mistook him for the best

Then I wandered into politics
And I let 'em touch my face
I lost not just my innocence
But my one slim chance of grace

So I sing these incantations
Revelations to no one
Yes I sing these incantations
To salvations come undone

Mother kept her Christmas cards
And the titles to our slaves
Wrote Pentecostal histories
In which we all were saved

We came from ancient nomad clans
And they kept careful track
But with the mess we've made here
They would never ask us back

So we sing these incantations
Revelations to no one
Yes we sing these incantations
To salvations come undone

Why are the children godless
And yet still speak in tongues?
These must be distant memories
Of when the world was young

I spent far too many mornings
Doing penance for my nights
Instead of asking for forgiveness
I kept asking for my rights

Now my only hope of happiness
Is to step right off this earth
And come back as a copperhead
Or pray for virgin birth

So I sing these incantations
Revelations to no one
Yes I sing these incantations
To salvations come undone

 ## C'est pas pour moi

C'est pas pour moi
Cette trop grande ville
J'suis un gars des ruelles
D'un village tranquille

Un petit paumé
Qui sait se dire Halte
Au premier pas
Sur vilain asphalte

J'ai grandi loin
De cette rouge lumière
Qui ronge le ciel
De vos rues guerrières

J'ai côtoyé
De ces naïves bêtes
Qu'affolent toujours
Les bruits de fête

C'est une petite histoire pathétique
À laquelle il ne manque que le romantique

On est donc arrivés en ville
Comme on tombe dans l'eau
Je fus bientôt seul
Dans ce froid Plateau

Il y a eu déception
Il y a pas eu mort
Mais vous conviendrez
Que j'ai pas eu tort

C'est pas pour moi
Cette trop grande ville
J'suis un gars des ruelles
D'un village tranquille

Un petit paumé
Qui aurait dû se dire Halte
Au premier pas
Sur ce vilain asphalte

Au premier pas
Sur ce vilain asphalte

 # It's Not For Me [C'est pas pour moi]

It's not for me
This too-big city
I'm a guy from the alleys
From a quiet small town

A little loser
Who knows to say Stop
At the first step
Onto nasty asphalt

I grew up far
From that red glow
That knaws the sky
Above your warring streets

I hung out with
The sort of naive outsiders
Who are always frightened
By party noise

It's a small pathetic story
Missing only romance

So we arrived in the city
Like falling into water
I was soon alone
In this cold Plateau

There was deception
There was no loss of life
But you'll agree
That I was not wrong

It's not for me
This too-big city
I'm a guy from the alleys
From a quiet small town

A little loser
Who should have said Stop
At the first step
Onto nasty asphalt

At the first step
Onto nasty asphalt

 # The Numbers

One flamenco dancer
Two homecoming queens
Three midwestern debutantes
Who weren't quite what they seemed

Four across the water
Who took me for a ride
One who knew the answer
And never left my side

I count the numbers
One by one
Love by love
'Til I'm done
'Til I'm done

I've got three to die for
One to keep alive
Three of the blood of my father
And all those close beside

Five true believers
Six already gone
Ten in foreign cities
Many close to home

I count the numbers
One by one
Love by love
'Til I'm done
'Til I'm done

Yes it really matters
This trail of lost and found
Each one leaves traces in my heart
Like footprints 'cross the ground
'Cross the ground..

There's a dozen on the corner
Fifty on their feet
Hundreds bright as shooting stars
Thousands marching in the street

Millions of the innocent
Legions of the poor
Thousands more who won't be back
Victims of our wars

I count the numbers
One by one
Love by love
I count the numbers
One by one
Love by love
'Til I'm done
'Til I'm done
'Til I'm done

Appendix A

Discography of Christopher Mark Jones recordings

No More Range to Roam (1978)

1   Dust To Dust (3:56)
2   Hard To Imagine (3:36)
3   Morning Glory (3:38)
4   Holy (2:40)
5   Steelhead Blues (3:24)
6   No More Range To Roam (3:38)
7   Whatever You Do (4:03)
8   The Road To Spain (3:07)
9   Baby Don't Go (4:28)
10 Ballerina (4:17)

Musicians:
- Christopher Mark Jones—acoustic guitar, piano, cello and vocals
- Jeffrey Jones—harmony vocals (1,3,4,5,6,8,9) acoustic guitar (7,8), piano (3,10), viola (2,7,10), harmonica (1) harmonium (6,8)
- Mick Linnard—bass (1,2,3,4,5,6,8,9), acoustic lead (3), 2nd acoustic (9,10)
- Pick Withers—drums (1,2,3,4,5,6,8,9)
- Gerald Moore—electric guitar (1, 2,5,6,9)

Produced by Christopher Mark Jones and Bill Leader. Recorded by Bill Leader at Leader Sound in Yorkshire, U.K., Oct.-Dec. 1977.

Notes: In the fall of '77, Bill Leader invited me to his studio in the Yorkshire Dales (U.K.) to make a album under his imprint for Transatlantic Records. My brother Jeffrey Jones, back-up guitarist Mick Linnard and I spent most of a week there, with early work from Dire Straits drummer Pick Withers, and a later visit from London guitarist Gerald Moore. The resulting recording was released in five countries and got me on prominent bills at folk festivals (Rotterdam, Bristol), and extensive radio play, including BBC1 and Capitol Radio in the U.K. In the intervening years Transatlantic and its catalogue disappeared in a series of mergers and acquisitions. The current version is remastered from the original vinyl, retaining the pristine sound of Bill's great mics and touch, while matching the levels and removing the clicks and pops.

Heartland Variations (2010)

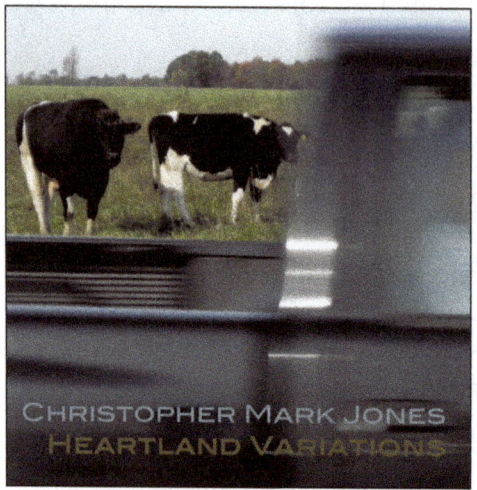

1. Black Earth (3:25)
2. Cincinnati Night (3:48)
3. Question of Style (3:26)
4. Uncertain Times (3:23)
5. Love's Not a Fashion (3:44)
6. Gas It Up (3:36)
7. Yes (4:15)
8. I Work Hard (For a Livin') (3:18)
9. Dakota Territory (3:25)

Musicians:
- Christopher Mark Jones —electric and acoustic guitar, electric bass, cello, drum programming (all)
- Jack Bowen—piano (8)
- Bev Futrell—harmonica (2), mandolin (3,6,9)
- David Gillespie—lead acoustic guitar (6)
- Jeffrey Jones—vocal harmony (1,2,3,5,6,7,8,9)
- Karen Jones—fiddle (7,9) vocal harmony (1,6,8)
- Mark Weakland—drums and percussion (all)

Produced and recorded by Christopher Mark Jones in Pittsburgh, Pennsylvania and Lexington, Kentucky from 2007-2009.

Notes: This is a catching-up album, including songs I'd had in my bag for awhile, which means they'd also stood the test of time. Exceptions are "Gas It Up," a song I wrote for Uptown Combo in 2006 or so, "I Work Hard," a tune reworked from a concept that had lain around waiting to be finished, and "Dakota Territory," written about the harsh upper Midwest of my forefathers. A lot of this work was done alone in my studio. The family contributions—Bev, David, Jeffrey, Karen—were overdubbed in Lexington. Mark came in when most of the rest had already been done.

Suburban 2-Step (2012)

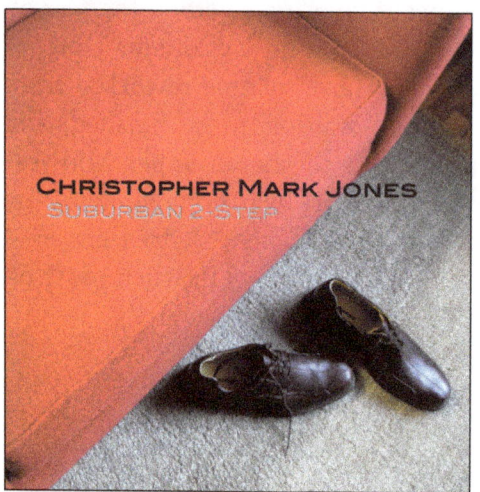

1	Home At Last	(3:30)
2	The Numbers	(3:50)
3	High	(4:01)
4	Autumn Song	(3:32)
5	Roseland	(4:06)
6	Montreal Again	(3:35)
7	Mrs. Pennington	(3:54)
8	Drivin'	(3:56)
9	Surburban 2-Step	(3:50)
10	Hoop Dreams	(4:19)
11	Rock County Line	(3:36)
12	The World Rolls On	(3:53)

Musicians:
- Christopher Mark Jones—lead vocals (all), harmony vocals (12), acoustic guitar (all), electric guitar (4), piano (3.7), organ (2,3,4)
- Roger Day—tuba (12)
- Paul Eiss—tenor (3) & soprano (12) sax
- Bev Futrell—vocal harmonies (8,12), mandolin (1,6,8,9) & harmonica (11)
- Dave Gillespie—vocal harmonies (1,2,3,5,6,9,10,12), acoustic (1,6,8) & electric (2,3,5,9,10) guitars

- David Hart—tres (2) & mandolin (12)
- Karen Jones—vocal harmonies (1,2,5,6,8,9,10,12) & fiddle (5,6,8,9)
- Regina Ketter—viola & violin (1,4,7)
- Gordon Kirkwood—cello (1,4,7)
- Marc Reisman—harmonica (5,10)
- Jim Spears—bass (1,2,3,4,5,6,9,10)
- Mark Weakland—drums (1,2,3,4,5,6,9,10)

Produced, arranged and recorded by Christopher Mark Jones from July-December 2011 in Pittsburgh and Detroit.

Notes: All of these songs were written in the two years prior to this recording, with the exception of "Roseland," which was written in the eighties and refers to living in central London (making some of the reference—the Circus, the Mall, kippers, the Underground etc—a bit more understandable; for a while afterwards). I brought in Jim Spears on bass this time, figuring I had enough to do, and a general studio upgrade allowed for recording the entire rhythm section (+ guide track) all at once, which I'm sure was easier for drummer Mark Weakland. This was my first time arranging strings, but I invoked the spirit of my father William (who was a PhD in music theory) and the advice of my brother Jeff. That and some contributions from Gina Ketter and Gordon Kirkwood resulted in an addition I like, especially when the arrangements are a bit sparse—"Autumn Song" and "Mrs. Pennington." I set up the studio for a weekend in my cousin Dave Gillespie's house in Detroit, and "family band" members Dave, Karen Jones, and Bev Futrell got a lot of their contributions down then, though Dave continued to send me guitar parts for a while after. Roger Day, Marc Reisman, David Hart, and Paul Eiss all came in on separate occasions to work their magic and spend a moment in the suburbs (though I don't remember any two-steps—must have missed them...).

Atlantica (2014)

1. Best I Got (3:26)
2. The Trapper's Wife (3:56)
3. The Blackstone Rangers (4:04)
4. Walkin' 19 (5:44)
5. Muffins (4:07)
6. Dans la Ville (3:08)
7. Miguel y Celestina (3:54)
8. Big Mac (4:45)
9. All They Seek (4:11)
10. Hockey Éternité (3:24)

Musicians:
- Christopher Mark Jones—lead vocals (all), harmony vocals (2,7), acoustic guitar (all), electric guitar (4)
- Brooke Annibale—harmony vocals (1,4,7)
- Autumn Ayers—harmony vocals (1,2,3,4,8,9)
- Vince Camut—pedal steel (1,2,7), electric guitar (6), dobro (3,5)
- Joe DeFazio—organ (4,8,9)
- David Hart—mandolin (1,2,7)
- Dave Gillespie—electric guitar (3,8,9), harmony vocals (7)
- Ben Shannon—harmony vocals (9)
- Jim Spears—bass (1,2,3,4,5,6,9,10)
- Mark Weakland—drums (1,2,3,4,5,6,9,10)

Produced, arranged and recorded by Christopher Mark Jones

from June 2013—March 2014 in Studio 256, Pittsburgh, Pennsyvania.

Notes: All are new songs, some written with the explicit intention of not being so (Americana) parochial, including one with my Quebec poet friend (and hockey player) Bernard Pozier. Most songs had various rhythms of the record laid down first with Mark and Jim, with other parts overdubbed. Autumn did the heavy lifting on harmony vocals this time, though it was great to have Ben and Brooke contribute as well. Joe DeFazio had done a sub gig for me back in Uptown Combo days, and proved to be adaptable to the various feels of this record. Vince played multiple instruments, and all with taste and restraint. Dave Gillespie drove down from Detroit for the weekend for his parts, and David Hart stopped over for a couple of evenings. Mixing and mastering mostly occurred in February and March, with constant redos until I finally just had to stop...

Incantations (2017)

1. The Fire So Soon (4:45)
2. What That Means (3:03)
3. Lordstown (3:40)
4. Incantations (4:12)
5. Bobby & Ginnie (4:45)
6. I'll Stay By Your Side (3:49)
7. Railway Track (3:56)
8. Field Of Dreams (3:51)
9. Kansas (2:49)
10. I Saw The Sea Come Slowly Rising (3:56)
11. Spoken For (5:00)
12. Don't Look Behind (4:34)
13. C'est Pas Pour Moi (2:45)

- Christopher Mark Jones—lead vocals (all), harmony vocals (1,3,8,10), acoustic guitar (all), high-strung guitar (10), piano (13)
- Vince Camut—pedal steel, electric & high-strung guitars, banjo (all)
- Mark Perna—upright & electric bass (all)
- Mark Weakland—drums (all)
- Markila (Kiki) Brown—vocal harmonies (4,6,12)
- Richard (Hutch) Hutchins—harmonies (4,6,12)

- Eric Kurtzrock—drums (10)
- Younga Reitz—cello (5,11)
- Skip Sanders—organ (1,3,4,7), piano (3,5,6,8,9,12), accordion (13)
- Sasha Shapiro—viola (9,11)
- Rachel Whitcomb—harmonies (3,5,8,9)
- Joyce Wohlgemuth—violin (5,11)

Produced, arranged and recorded by Christopher Mark Jones from October 2015—December 2016 at Studio 256, Pittsburgh, Pennsylvania.

Notes: Most of the tracks had been laid down in the new home of Studio 256 by the end of the summer of 2017, with mixing spread out over September and October, and mastering beginning in November and completed in December. The core recordings were done by the Roots Ensemble (Camut, Perna, Weakland) with Hammond organ happening at Skip Sander's studio, then piano, strings (arranged by brother Jeffrey Jones) and harmonies. One of the themes in the writing was movement and change through generations, another constancy in love.

About the Author

Christopher Mark Jones

The songwriter saga pretty much started in Paris about 1976, when Christopher found that all he wanted to do was sing and play guitar. He had spent a half-dozen years playing professional basketball (in Portugal) and studying languages (Portuguese, French, Spanish) and was enrolled at the National Institute for Oriental Languages and Civilizations in Paris at the time where he was studying Chinese. He coasted to a degree in that program, while playing in restaurants and the Metro, then headed out for London to do music full-time, joining a friend of his in a squat in Central London. The folk revival was going full-speed in the UK, and there were lots of clubs where you could go do three songs for free and have some chance of being hired back for a few quid. He also got a regular gig at Bunjies, a tiny little club in the West End. He met a Welshman named Mick Linnard, a guitarist who enjoyed playing his tunes, and they became traveling partners. He played a showcase spot at the Cambridge Folk Festival, where a singer named Rosie Hardman heard him and recommended him to Bill Leader, a legendary producer (Bert Jansch, John

Renbourne and Nic Jones among others), who had a deal with Transatlantic Records to issue records under his imprint.

The album they did together (see Recordings) with contributions from Mick, Christopher's brother Jeff, Gerald Moore, who was a popular club guitarist in London and Pick Withers on drums (Dire Straits) had some success. The album was licensed in five countries in Europe and getting some decent reviews, but it came out at the same time that punk hit in London, and the reception for acoustic songwriters was at an all-time low in the UK.

After moving back to the US in 1979, he had a look at the potential for work in the Boston area, and started putting together a band, mostly called the Regulars, which worked consistently for several years with excellent musicians (Andre Locke of Mandrake, Reeves Gabrels who ended up with David Bowie's Tin Machine) and paid starvation wages.

When he and wife Linda had two sons, Tanner and Max, he turned his language background into a Ph.D in French literature and became a very part-time musician until they left home. He taught at Bentley College in Waltham, then Carnegie Mellon in Pittsburgh, where he stayed for 25 years, doing research in the French-speaking cultures of the world (especially popular music) and developing technology-enhanced language courses.

In roughly 2002, he started playing regularly with a couple of NYC expats named Jonah Winters (clarinet) and Sally Denmead, (cigar-box uke) who had a fetish for Tin Pan Alley tunes from the 30s and 40s. The tunes had lots of changes, he got some guitar chops back together and eventually moved on to playing more blues and jazz-based material with Jack Bowen on piano and Jim Spears on base in a group they called the Uptown Combo. That allowed him to spread out on guitar and learn a whole catalogue of new tunes--never a bad thing. When he had assembled the digital toybox needed to do an album for the Uptown Combo, he got the acoustic guitar out and realized that he'd like to do some recording of original material as well. The resulting album—"Heartland Variations"—signified a singer-songwriter renaissance. He then re-mastered the Transatlantic (UK) album "No More Range to Roam," which is now available on CD. Three additional recordings of new songs have since followed, including "Suburban 2-Step," released in April of 2012, 2014's "Atlantica" and 2017's "Incantations."

While he continues to travel and perform in formats ranging from solo to full band, he is also working with songwriter friends to promote concerts in Pittsburgh and is working on a variety of projects in his own studio as both producer and engineer.

For updated information on performances and recordings, go to: christophermarkjones.com.

www.ingramcontent.com/pod-product-compliance
Lightning Source LLC
Chambersburg PA
CBHW080515110426
42742CB00017B/3116